Big!

Explorer Challenge

Which toy has these round ears?

OXFORD
UNIVERSITY PRESS

Retell the Story

Look at the pictures and retell the story in your own words.

Look Back, Explorers

What are Lee and Kipper doing?

Look at page 4. What does Kipper imagine the hippo is doing?

Why is it funny that the ant is bigger than the dinosaur (on pages 8–9)?

Did you find out which toy has these round ears?

Explorer Challenge: the mouse (page 5)

What's Next, Explorers?

Now find out about big and small animals ...

Explorer Challenge
for *As Big As Me!*

What animal is this?